# The Custom House

POETRY BY DENNIS DALY

IBBETSON STREET PRESS

©2012 Dennis Daly
Book and cover design by S. Glines

Ibbetson Street Press
25 School Street
Somerville MA 02143

www.ibbetsonpress.com

ISBN 978-0-9846614-1-1

All rights reserved including the right to reproduce this work in any form except as provided by U.S. Copyright law.
For information contact the publisher.

Ibbetson Street Press Printing June 2012
Printed in the United States of America

*Typography*
text: Bauer Bodoni
titles: Caslon Antique

For Joanne,
who saved many
of these poems
from time's little
conflagrations

Also by Dennis Daly

**Sophocles' Ajax**
a *translation*, (2012, Wilderness House Press)

**10X3**
Poems by Robert De Young, Dennis Daly,
and Patrick Duddy
Poets at Northeastern Series No. 8

# CONTENTS

## I. THE CUSTOM HOUSE

| | |
|---|---|
| On the Seawall | 3 |
| The Custom House | 4 |
| Off Boone Island | 5 |
| The Boat | 6 |
| Babur's Garden | 8 |
| Jogging in Kabul | 10 |
| At the Mustapha Hotel | 11 |
| The Tunnel | 12 |
| Qala-i-Jangi | 14 |
| The Dogs of Mazar-i-Sharif | 16 |
| Hekmatyar | 18 |
| Landmines | 19 |
| Last Caravan | 20 |
| Samarkand | 21 |
| The Bug Pit | 22 |
| Daniel's Tomb | 23 |
| Two Bullet Holes | 24 |
| The Fish | 25 |
| In the Pesticide Desert | 27 |
| A Boy Banging a Drum | 28 |
| Diyarbakir 2003 | 29 |
| The Cooking Pot | 30 |
| Sakaeo | 31 |
| Khmer Rouge | 32 |
| The Seamstress of Nom Samet | 33 |

## II. DANCING WITH MY DAUGHTERS

| | |
|---|---|
| Dancing with my Daughters | 37 |
| A Plea for Protection | 39 |
| Boy in a Gray Windbreaker | 41 |
| Telegraph Line | 42 |
| Rowboat At Embden Pond | 43 |
| Rosary | 44 |
| Concussion in Winter | 45 |

| | |
|---|---|
| Beth | 46 |
| A Bucket of Flounder | 47 |
| Scarlet Fever | 48 |
| In the Light Bulb Graveyard | 49 |
| Dublin Wedding | 50 |
| Leaving Paris | 52 |
| Your Study | 53 |
| The Violinist | 55 |
| Playing Chess with Jim | 56 |
| Epithalamium | 57 |
| Philoctetes' Foot | 58 |
| The Catch | 59 |
| Peace | 60 |
| Francis | 62 |
| Chasing the Moon | 63 |
| Caesarian Birth | 64 |
| Fallstaff Reminisces | 65 |
| Mermaid's Purse | 66 |
| "I Thought All for the Best" | 67 |
| Vertigo | 68 |
| Night Café | 69 |
| Moon Path | 70 |
| Night Crawlers | 71 |
| New World | 72 |

## III. INDUSTRIAL SONNETS

| | |
|---|---|
| In Building 30 | 75 |
| Retirement | 76 |
| The Bench Hand | 77 |
| The Foreman | 78 |
| Security Guards | 79 |
| The Oil Farm | 80 |
| The Fork Lift | 81 |
| The Steward | 82 |
| Election Night at Union Hall | 83 |
| The Welder | 84 |
| Tool Keepers | 85 |

The Custom House

| | |
|---|---|
| The Auditors | 86 |
| Time Clock | 87 |
| Piece Work | 88 |
| In the Scrap Yard | 89 |
| Unemployment Line | 90 |
| The Cutter of Fiber Glass | 91 |
| The Vendors | 92 |
| Lovers above the Resin Silos | 93 |
| Wildcat Strike | 94 |
| Overtime | 95 |
| Maintenance | 96 |
| Asbestos | 97 |
| Benefits | 98 |
| Drill Smoke | 99 |
| Gear Plant Gate | 100 |
| The Carboloy Insert | 101 |
| Layoff | 102 |
| Rat-Friend | 103 |
| The Electrician | 104 |

## Previously Published Poems

On the Seawall — Soundings East Vol. 1 No. 1
Vertigo — Poetry & Vol. 1 No. 3
Mermaid's Purse — Boston Today Magazine Dec. 1978
In Building 30 — Tendril No. 16
Retirement — Tendril No. 16
The Bench Hand — Tendril No. 16
The Foreman — Tendril No. 16
Security Guards — Tendril No.16
The Oil Farm — Tendril No. 16
Dancing with my Daughters — The Lyric Vol. 63 No. 4
Night Cafe — The Sou'wester Vol. 3 No.1
Caesarian Birth — Lyrical Somerville Vol. 40 No. 1
"I Thought All for the Best" — 10 X 3 Chapbook
Telegraph Line — Muddy River Poetry Review Spring 2012
Samarkand — Muddy River Poetry Review Spring 2012
The Boat — Istanbul Literary Review 2012
Diyarbakir 2003 — Istanbul Literary Review 2012
Jogging in Kabul — Istanbul Literary Review 2012
Your Study — Istanbul Literary Review 2012
The Electrician — Istanbul Literary Review 2012
Beth — Bagels with the Bards Anthology #7
The Cooking Pot, Chasing the Moon
— Wilderness House Literary Review Vol 6 No 4

# The Custom House
## POETRY BY DENNIS DALY

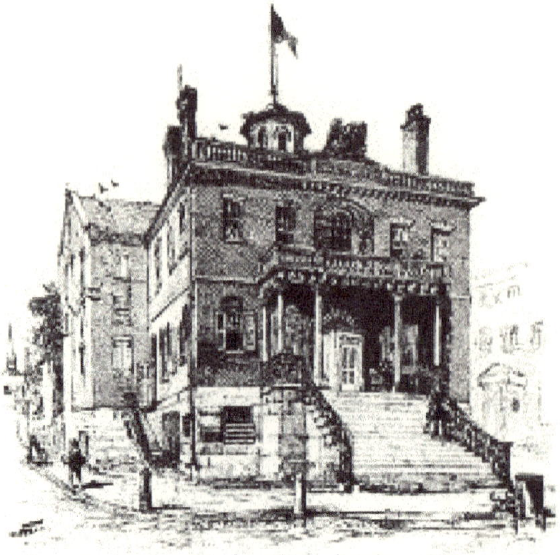

# I. THE CUSTOM HOUSE

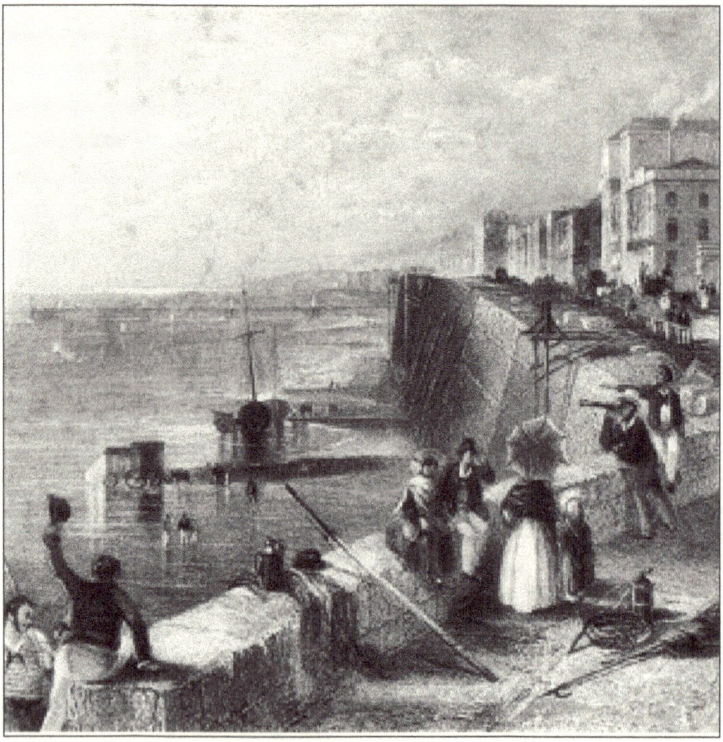

The Custom House

## On the Seawall

Attack of the hurricane steeds, the surge
So overpowering they burst back
Against their own, ripping up the soft

Strand of beach, sending pebbles of sand
And seaweed rags upward through the froth-violence.
Again the wall holds: its throaty cries,

A gurgle of blood, rising to a new pitch,
Bracing for the next assault; they come
In threes. The first: iron-plaited, basher-

Of-stone; the next two: dismantled
Grinders, nibblers at a fat-fleshed
Belly. Another three. And another.

A solitary monster on occasion
Powers in, climbing the backs
Of lesser waves, nourishing
Immensity, its giant jaws poised:
Eater-of-concrete, flooder-of-causeway.
These are the waves to watch.

Dennis Daly

# The Custom House

Another age: our greed- governed ancestors
Venture forth, significant super cargoes
Compelling the twins: speed and economy.
They bounded oceans for Madagascar
Or Malay, craved the Orient's garb.

We watch for their return with telescope
Of brass: pennants streaming, hull stowed with teas
And silks. We dream them into our harbors.
We await tribute from captains now arrived,
Long doldrumed—their ships in need of repair:
Sails split and rotting, spars sprung.

Ascending the granite steps, these dangerous men,
These men unable to meet our tariffs
Curse the collectors of the world, the weights
And measures; their minds unbalanced, salt-eaten.
They sulk impatiently, clawing their daggers:
We've seen their kind before.

Once in every while a revolution;
They murder us at our desks: stabbed with pen,
Bludgeoned with ink bottle. We disappear
For a time: there are advantages,
Our ghostly machinery still keeping account.
In the end they always pay.

## OFF BOONE ISLAND

Up-thrust swells so high
The periscope gadget
So smartly rigged up
To mast fails to see
Beyond the next wave
Beyond the pressure vaults
Where a man if fallen
Veers away, away
To ever, a place
Of bobbing; life pressed
In a vise of salt spray
Straddling the world
Of nether, never
Seen, a fugitive
Outside bluff boundary
Of mind and battered
Boat. I see myself
Deepening into
The cleft of waters
Into the very
Hoarseness of heaven's
Ecstatic death-buzz.

Dennis Daly

## The Boat

Toward open sea, the boat plunged on blue;
Its white wings part of a persistent wind.
Brine-crusted faces kept to the horizon
Blanking out burnt ships, a charred city.
Tautness held slave to their turgid sails,
They tacked from the harbor leaving death behind.

Cut off from their own kind, kin fallen behind;
Fallen in the blood-dust, bodies disease-blue.
Billboards proclaim, "Deep freezers on sale—
When the cure is found, awake to the wind."
And all around stench curls through the city;
Time frozen at the wrong time: misplaced horizons.

Buildings bulb up through broken horizons
Following men, who dare not look behind,
Down crooked streets in the gargoyle city.
The mid-day sun on bowsprit glares blue.
Pestilence rides in the radiant wind;
The remnant die, only few have set sail.

The harbor cleared, boat under full sail:
World-Weary, the crew labors, seeks the horizon.
Both life and death bringing, came the tepid wind;
Heat pressed to brains, memories lost, left behind.
Days gone, years crushed between planes of blue;
Clothed in scaled skin: spilt oils in a doomed city.

The Custom House

Towers are seen. Towers of a city!
Confusion on deck: toward these towers they sail;
They greet the gulls squawking in the sky's blue.
White walls rise up on a green horizon,
A breathing wood; gulls call from behind.
Wrong! Something is wrong. They awake to the wind.

Luffed sails, all quiet but the wind.
Fruit trees ripen over white-walled city,
Grape vines to fences cling; young women behind:
Nudes in the sun. Men watch the strange sails;
They fish the lagoon, blind to the blind horizon.
No sound or ripple on the sea's blue.

Cursing reefs and wind, the boatmen sail;
Prow dips west: the riddle of horizon.
No sound or ripple on the sea's blue.

Dennis Daly

## Babur's Garden

Pomegranates and citrons, lemons,
Sour cherries and a banana tree,
Which unexpectedly thrived; fountains
Of diverted water, a beauty

So fertile, you gushed, so temperate.
The sugar cane planted earlier,
Sent to Badakhshan and Bukhara's market
Places. For sweetness nothing worthier

From Eastern climes. All this on a rise
Overlooking the steady river flow
South of Kabul's fortress. The sharp skies
Warming leaves and channels of rainbow.

Surely descended from Timur
And your mother insists from Jengis,
You are the conqueror, the unsure
King of cities, who with a brief kiss

Took Ferghana, blinked, and was gone.
Samarkand submitted to you thrice
But your armies outnumbered, again withdrawn
Into the hills like scurried mice

Seeking safety from the Uzbek rage
Until you reigned over this pliant city.
And here with your book of self, the page
Again turns. Horse archer without pity

The Custom House


Now you lie in a clover meadow
Surrounded by orange trees, their orbs
Just turning yellow, a fine plateau—
Your favorite place that nicely absorbs

The heat of responsibility
Into the pooled water of life's landscape,
The churning dreams and the poetry.
You write again, there is no escape

From your vision of high empire years,
Golden villages sacked, forward movement
Of men and cannon, allaying fears:
The collapse of the war- elephant.

Dennis Daly

## Jogging in Kabul

Running through the cratered streets
Will not do anymore, a bomb
On the course, no note of ransom
Needed, a lot longer life beats

Out the thrill of breathlessness.
We move to the city's outskirts,
Our adrenaline sport of flirts
And flight territorially less

Likely to ball us in blue flames
Of pity. Howls of Afghan laughter
Translate, caress this dead center
Of mine detection, our surnames

Hawk wings to locals. Unanchored
We run for our reedy-thin lives
Among the faux mines, absent wives
And husbands remote ideas, a hoard

Of liquor, love's angry questions
Waiting for us, like a sub-text
Wondering where to step next,
We wince, defer all decisions.

## AT THE MUSTAPHA HOTEL

Thursday night they barbeque on the roof
Overlooking Kabul; the plastic chairs
And tables set up, above the nightmares
Of neighborhood. The hotel is bombproof,

They joke: its walls are partitions of glass.
I'm told the UN people like it here.
The Germans just installed a tap for beer.
At the downstairs bar we're at an impasse

Over my travel plans in the Hindu Kush.
Weis, the bartender, nods, agrees with me.
You'll make it to the tunnel, then maybe,
If they let you right through, you'll miss the ambush

In bandit country. You're not serious
Said another: Up there it's certain death;
At that altitude not a bloody breath
Comes easily. Don't be unconscious

To danger; Overland you cannot go
Unless in military convoy.
We left next morning with no scheme or decoy,
Heading north to blown bridges and blasted snow.

Dennis Daly

# The Tunnel

Past the line of opium trucks
High in the Hindu Kush Mountains
Above the flight of watchful falcons,
Here in the birthplace of epochs,

We drove up to a flimsy gate
Where two guards demanded papers, signed
By some authority aligned
With tribe: a signature and a date.

I had a yes, a written okay
Of presidential protection.
But passage was not for foreign
Whims; they blocked the bombed-out thruway.

The radio man wheezed a message
To find his Tajic commander,
Who, clomping in like a centaur,
Demanded his rightful homage.

He came with the construction boss,
A Turk, the engineer of record.
I'm here, I lied to the warlord,
To inspect, then to double-cross

Your tunnel, both up to Mazar
And back again in a few days.
The job you're doing, I'll appraise;
Your pay I'll make an urgent matter.

They opened the gate; we drove through.
Steno pad in hand, I noted flaws:
Enormous potholes, which gave pause—
Our auto barely making-do.

The Custom House

In the dark, nods of approval
Aimed at us from commander and staff.
Now I must say on my behalf:
This deception was most useful.

Before we had left I was told
Get through it, that's bandit country,
To go around is foolhardy.
In these tall mountains, men are stone-cold

Killers, only the blown tunnel
Saved the Russians and even Masood,
The hammer unseen and unsubdued,
From slaughter, from this set anvil

Of eternal war, where foes collide
And after kin, a multiple
Of murder. A blinding medal
Of light meets us on the other side.

Dennis Daly

## Qala-i-Jangi

They expected me. The garrison turned out,
Before I was driven in. Staked out banners
Praised the glorious dead with words, no doubt,
Well meant. The commander showing his manners,

Offered a meal; I accepted only tea.
Then the obligatory tour of the fort:
The neat pile of used shells, a wall still bloody
From frantic hands that could not push off or thwart

Or hide from the fierce and undeterred stalk
Of utter darkness. The craters were still there
And the roofless pink house; we stopped our walk,
Looked into the broken, underground lair,

Where the final stand of insurrection
Was bombed and burned and flooded into shock.
The survivors from this torturous bastion
Staggered up, bone-cold, unable to talk

Sense or see a future; they were trucked away.
We moved on to the American's shrine
A cenotaph of sorts, a tasteful cliché.
He had begun to interrogate, define

His subjects, when hell came looking for him
As it does in this country. I felt rage,
Saw him cut down by the multitude, a grim
Reminder that man's vengeance and outrage

The Custom House

Cannot be ignored, or cowed into place.
Our stern commander nodded at one ghost
And I knew he had the power to erase,
To override. Then this errant shadow-host

Smiled at me, as if to plead a lost case.
At that moment I saw the fortress anew,
Understood the commander's eerie face,
Felt the dread come for me, lay siege, break through.

Dennis Daly

## The Dogs of Mazar-i-Sharif

Through the entrance, the archway of city,
Into the dusty depression of crowd,
The muted sun descending like a shroud.
Nearby the blue mosque of Hazrat Ali

Quivers in the heat, a counterfeit some say
To hide the ancient tomb of Zoroaster,
Whose god granted will, not the disaster
Of chaos and conquest, a warrior's way.

My driver dropped me at the Mazar Hotel.
It was empty, and seedy, and cavernous.
At ten I left my room and stepped, anxious,
Down the grand staircase, a walk to repel

Some doubt, an aching, forgotten worry.
Out the back door into a garden, I paced
Past fruit trees, the evening air cool, a taste
Of Eden. I jumped over boundary,

A low wall, and headed toward somewhere
Alive with brash laughter and neon light.
On a nondescript street, no traffic in sight,
Uneasily I walked; something in the air

Bothered me, brought into single focus
A forlorn howl from some beast up ahead.
I trod on, a new fear forming, unsaid.
Now others joined in ungentle chorus.

From behind a dumpster, then on balcony,
Then in the darkest alley I heard them
By the hundreds, a howling of mayhem:
Each outdoing the other, an envy

The Custom House


Of higher notes, an uncanny, savage crave,
Unearthly to my nervous ear. I stood still
For a moment, an effort to distill
My building terror back to reason, outbrave

What could not be: a city lost by night
To wolves, whose packs, gone ravenous, roam free.
I turned, imagined leveled, fiery
Eyes following my retreat, my controlled flight

Back to the hotel and armed security.
I heard the tale of horror months later.
When the Taliban took the city, anger
Overflowed. They ordered blood-barbarity

Against the Mongol Hazareas. The outrage began
As door to door they slaughtered them where they stood,
Dragging them into the street like firewood.
And there they remained by decree. No Afghan

Could touch them on pain of execution.
The starved city-dogs came out and feasted.
The howling that I'd heard was the cry of those cheated
Animals, recalling their lost fortune.

## Hekmatyar

Majahideen shape-shifter, you haunt
The Nuristan hills, hawk-eyed, depraved
Primate of war's gnashing and blood flaunt.
You got religion young and engraved

Unveiled faces with your acid
Attacks at Kabul University.
The Russian officers you tortured
And skinned in some creepy repartee:

Center stage before a tank convoy.
You sated on American money
But hated that supercool cowboy
Can-do face. Your temper: downright cagey.

You shelled Masood and the capitol
Destroying your own true believers.
Now you're Taliban, beyond brutal—
A goblin, one with all deceivers.

The Custom House

## Landmines

The drunk de-miner downs his beer,
Numbs his nerves, outthinks tomorrow;
Men mine the world to kill their fear.

He works alone; he tries to clear
From hidden nook the dire gizmo;
The drunk de-miner downs his beer.

Our amputees are not so dear
To us it seems—the new credo:
Men mine the world to kill their fear.

A child with one leg seems sincere,
He offers help; he's one to know.
The drunk de-miner downs his beer.

Unmapped plots that do not cohere:
A killing field, a serpent's borough.
Men mine the world to kill their fear.

For arms dealers a new good year;
Bank accounts filled in vile escrow.
The drunk de-miner downs his beer;
Men mine the world to kill their fear.

Dennis Daly

## Last Caravan

Strung across the great desert
Like minute paper cutouts,
Camels trod in dire effort
Between oases, long bouts

Of blazing sun, firing
The morning air with waves of burn;
They cross this world with stubborn
Rhythm, bundles high riding

Against the lined horizon.
These Kuchi-led beasts of dune
To the grim winds throw caution:
Their dreamtime-span closing soon.

The Custom House

## Samarkand

Over the rolling hills
Into a denial of setting.
One of Alexander's armies
Dropped through the earth's crust
Nearby. His generals sworn
To secrecy. A defeat
Expunged with meticulous
Care. The Macedonian
Host stalled. Roxanne's
People, sly and insinuating
Themselves into the continent's
Command. Such is the nature
Of the place. Timur ruled
His geography from here.
Others looked to the stars,
Observed the vast celestial globes
Turning their faces away
Retreating from our miniscule
Lives, our universes of indecision
Pent up, pressured, sprung back
Into a reassuring denseness
Encompassing all becomings.
A new dimension birthed by fire,
The etched map on an antique wall
Drawn to perfect scale, scars,
Angling toward the center of pulse and breath,
Arrows a way home.

Dennis Daly

## The Bug Pit

It's all a great game
Until Bukhara, the veiled
City of saints, captures you
In its crumbling Ark,
A fortress once holding the lost
Library of antiquity—a poetry
Of science muted, a music
Of sacred numbers, mulled
For a time, now unremembered.

Thrown into the verminous pit
Of viper heads to stomp
And flying jaws of bloodthirsty
Insects to swat and smash
Against the earthen wall,
You live only at the emir's
Pleasure. One day lying
In silk sheets, nursed
And salved, the next lowered
Into torment, a piece
By piece dissection until
The final outrage—a beheading
Or ad-libbed bafflement: a lifetime
Of knowledge now seeping through,
guttering into the glass grains
Of a desert's finished surface.

The Custom House

## DANIEL'S TOMB

After the steppes of undulation
Down the entry road of pervading dust
We found a hilltop shrine: spare, august
Beside a somber stream—a prophet's bastion.

Sufi holy men squatted, maintained guard
Over Daniel's relics, stolen long ago
By Tamerlane, who longed for charms to show
His horde that even bones of high regard

Urged him on to heights of world dominion.
Here we summoned words, began to pray,
Ask protection in the usual way
Against ferocity and sly brethren.

When done we tip the Muslim imams.
Said one: the saint grows each year, the tomb expands;
We build and build again with our own hands.
Then proffers a proof—his upturned calloused palms.

Dennis Daly

## Two Bullet Holes

Two bullet holes through
Our front windshield—
Redundant markings;
Other cars here much
The same, a local
Joke identified?
Our Russian Lada,
A dependable
Box. The driver does
Not want to leave yet
For Khiva until
Three. It's death, he says,
The desert heat can
Kill. He's right, of course,
But I argue for
One, not wanting to lose
The day. He's upset
But agrees. We leave
To find bottles of
Water, load the car,
Leave into the heat.
A landscape of blister
Bends toward the horizon,
Etched into coarseness
Of crenulated
Dune and dirt-streaked ridge.
The destination
Of our journey loses
All meaning in this
The in-between time,
The time that will find
New definition
In our rising thirst.

## THE FISH

Carjacked in Karalpakistan
Below the basin, where the Aral
Sea used to be, with my daughter,
Our driver co-opted
By two policemen in need
Of a ride home; seventy
Miles later, past yurts,
Through Nukus, the infamous
Headquarters of biological
Warfare, searching for a fish
In a desert fish-market
In some out-of-the-way
Village near the Oxus.
The fish we find
Is three feet long.
They lay it in the trunk
Of our subcompact
Russian car on top
Of our knapsacks, pleased
With themselves. Twenty
More miles. I've had it. Tell
Them to get out I rage
To our driver. No
He says, militsia, trouble.
I pull out an old ID badge
With a star on it, point
To myself, lie: US militsia
I say. They frown for a minute
Consider this; now
There are only two possibilities.
They choose the second
Of them, apologize
Over and over—a hint
Of what might have happened.

Dennis Daly

They remove their fish
And other belongings, bow
To us on the roadside
As we leave them behind.
I calm down and know
With dawning certainty
The fool that I am.

The Custom House

## In the Pesticide Desert

A hollow haze over arcs us.
We walk between the sunken boats,
The bluff where the canneries
Operated and warehouses stored

The salted fish products a mile
Away. A truck farther on roils up
A make-shift road cut diagonally
Across the arid bed of ancient bay,

Pulls to one side. Now two men looking
As they pretend to fix a break part
Or something in the axle. They glance
Again, measure us as future prey.

The unsettled dust, drained from cotton
Fields, deposited here, poisoning
The sea's lower fathoms, pernicious
Wet years loosed into earth's croaking breath.

Dennis Daly

## A Boy Banging a Drum

Spanning the Tigris
A Roman bridge built near-
By the black basalt walls
Of antiquity's realm.
A boy strides down the road
Banging a drum. Up on
The hill a restaurant
Where we'll eat course after
Course near Attaturk's house—
A museum, I think.
No one to open up.
We park, proceed over
To the river's other
Side: myself, two Kurdish
Partisans. Fiery swords
Quelled now. Fruit trees cut down.
The garden bulldozed, bare,
Divinely salted. Path
Leading south to where once
A man and his lover ruled
In vine-lush ignorance.

## DIYARBAKIR 2003

Straight razor to my throat
This Kurdish barber joked
At my expense—the room,
Crowded, with laughter boomed

And I joined in, good naturedly
I thought, or did not choose to see.
My rebel guides had brought me here
From the demonstration site near

The city center. The leaders
Arrested, we cleared out—cheaters
Of danger, through back doors and alley,
Into friendly homes we sallied

In retreat, the helicopter
Gunship high above. We hopped
Into our car. At the airport
Men in black suits arrived, the sort

That bring breaking news, a parliament's
Refusal of foreigner's bent
To pass through their country, to invade.
A debt here deferred, now unpaid.

## The Cooking Pot

Disinterred by some wretched boy
It collected the helpless fragments
Of humankind from the burnt-out valleys
And held them by a gravity,

Stronger than blood. Without it they died,
Bark- gnawing in the forests, starving
In the paddies, unable to make
Edible the gut-tearing plants.

After a while, their bellies filled, they
Marveled at its texture, the beauty
Of its hollowed-out, its reasoned shape.
In the end they worshipped it.

The Custom House

## SAKAEO

There on the peneplain we maintain
The meticulous ones, the estranged
Murderers, killers of their own kin;
They are penned together: family, friends—
A beaten soldiery of blank stares, of lost limbs.

Often the night nudges one or two
Awake and a moan breaks through their sweat,
A malaria sweat and we think
We hear remorse. It is not. It's joy:
A vivid moment, a remembrance

Of massacre—throat slashed or clubbing death.
Then they sleep again their fevered sleep.
Only morning, dissembling, dares them
To rise, like a mother, who will not nurse her child.
This is, of course, a camp of orphans.

Barbed wire merely pantomimes necessity;
Ever alert, they guard themselves all too well.

## KHMER ROUGE

Beaten, the wolf lies down, offers its throat.
The other, confused for the moment,
Backs away; there is chaos in the land.
All instinct defers to the one yielded,
Bars slaughter. But then, clean and razor
Sharp, the truth appears like a cache
Of gleaming well-tooled weapons, or the prodigious
Fangs of a primitive animal. Victory will
Never be enough; the only power
Which governs, governs through definition.
And defining oneself as deficient, empty,
Defines one's brothers. War for them was the attempt
To heal that insufferable hurt, a surgical
Cutting out of context, a subtraction, a lunge.

## The Seamstress of Nom Samet

Dried blood at the heart of the crystal,
An imperfection, a carbon spot:
Her means of livelihood glowered
Like a stunted god, whose black
Enameled surface spits askance
The bitterness of light.

We ate in a secret medieval
World surrounded by the impaled,
A hell of whispered, despairing cries.
When she laughed her eyes hardened
Like pieces of dry, burning ice,
Her lips too soft for words.

As noiselessly as angels of death
Her two sisters moved past us to the hut's
Entrance, greeting each lethal visitor,
Each carrier of darkness.
Only the clanking of their metal
Weapons cut the quiet.

A shadow had followed these refugees,
More ominous than a rising wind,
Stalked them for their soul's fabric, its formless
Breath. She breathed terror into their midst,
Mending her black pajama-like cloth,
Plotting destruction.

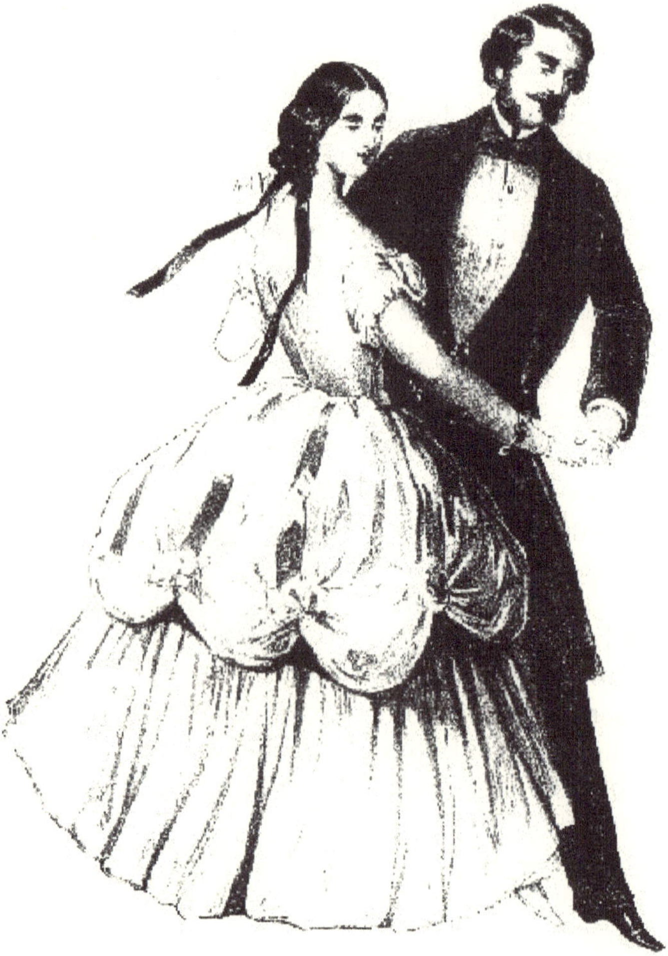

*II. DANCING WITH MY DAUGHTERS*

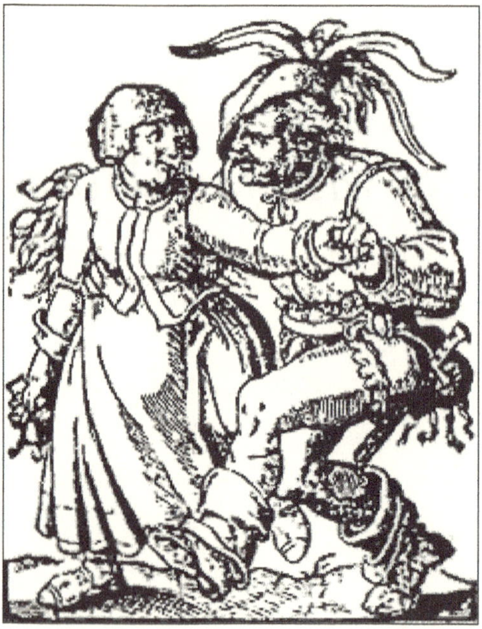

## DANCING WITH MY DAUGHTERS

Dancing with my daughters
Dancing with my dears;
Pipes and drums play in their hearts,
Quell their evening tears
Quell their evening tears.

One I cradle in my arms
The others hold my knee
Our song sung round the living room,
A whirling symmetry
A whirling symmetry.

We bump into a table
The needle skips a beat
The record ends, a strange silence;
It slows the dancer's feet
It slows the dancer's feet.

Soon the music starts again
An elegy or hymn;
A laugh, those tears, a smile combine
To rhyme what was a whim
To rhyme what was a whim.

Now sorrow fades to distance
We frolic in the fore;
These counterpoints of rhythm
Define our metaphor
Define our metaphor.

Dennis Daly

In jigs we step of moments
In reels we course through days
Our lifelong dance, love's measurement
We cannot paraphrase
We cannot paraphrase.

Dancing with my daughters
Dancing with my dears;
Pipes and drums play in their hearts,
Quell their evening tears
Quell their evening tears.

The Custom House

## A PLEA FOR PROTECTION
*version from the Irish of Muireadach O'Dalaigh, early 13th century.*

Fragile hand of youth, highborn, half-Gael,
We, the guests of your clan-house, greet you.
From what far land do they come, you ask,
Who governs? Listen, no gabble you'll hear.

Oft times with high powers we've quaffed our wine:
Monarch, nobility, God's own abbot.
We drink a mannered drink without blow
Or buffet; our song a peerless tune.

Each good verse an instrument of touch,
A knob into the tear-catching heart,
The swollen heart, haven of memory.
O bard, O poet, another, they shout.

But need I recount their flattery,
Their praise, number their bountiful gifts.
No. Others will sing of the heights attained,
Of my feats, my fame—tales you'll soon hear,

More seemly heard in their songs, not mine.
Just Lord of Leinster, brave protector,
We come to you from under the feet
Of Conn's children; our flight, we hope, finished.

The anger of Donnel pursues us,
His wrath unbounded. Yet this stern prince
Of the north would not abandon one,
O Fitzwilliam, who stood bold against you.

The quarrel itself: too trifling to tell.
I axed a churl, a tithe collector
Who abused my name. The puffed-up fool!
Should this—mere reflex—sire such enmity?

Dennis Daly

Lord of Tara, champion our cause.
There is no chessboard without a king,
No bard without a faultless patron.
Your name will be famous forever.

From the five provinces they will come,
The best poets of the Gaelic race,
For I am Muireadhach, bard of Meath.
Do not doubt: my verses are heeded.

## Boy in a Gray Windbreaker

Beyond the soccer field, the woods
Whistled alive, lifted branches
Through the speckled air, feathered darts
Flying the gale's torqued stream torrents.

He steps into it, his new gray
Jacket, his first new anything
Catches wind, forwards him, soars him
Into life's tempest: uprooted

Trees, airborne missiles drawn through, pulled
Plied together, mulching dead space
With his draft-tossed name, hurricane
Above his awed head, a shoulder slash,

A dub. Running now, up the path.
Siblings huddled in the cellar.
His future set, a destiny
Of storm, a birth from turbulence.

## Telegraph Line

My breath hesitated, over
And over in stuttered notes,
Connected with you in some
Bond of adolescent intensity
Lived between telegraph dots
And dashes. Your father ran
The line from your bedroom
In the project, across back-
Yards and stockade fence
To my soon-to-be-torn-down house.
We used toggle switches to send
And receive the dramatic
Messages of war and peace,
Of secret armies massing
Beyond the soccer field and sumac
Groves, where enemy forts
Guarded the outskirts of day-
Dreamed estates. Vineyards
Of deep blue concord grapes
Were grabbed and gorged by us.
Grateful to the easy gods
Of languor, we exchanged plans
Of epic lives and deft maturity.
One day our line failed. Your breath
Hesitated, over and over
In stuttered notes, you railed
At the lost current, the broken words,
The mimicry of two skewed worlds.

The Custom House

## ROWBOAT AT EMBDEN POND

Somewhere in the white eternal noise
Of space Mary-Lou bounces a laugh
At her buoyant brothers—the haughty boys
Of pond hyperbole. Each hold a staff

Of fury to face down a future
Armada, to command insurrection
Beyond this seeming ship of nature
Tree-tied. Oar-locks curling a question

Always here and there. The splash and squeal
Caught on kodachrome, never fading.
The final dive, surface slap, appeal
For applause, in sun's soft shading

Of morning: a bright happiness lost
As it happens. The sinking rowboat
Unbailed, in cosmic water storm-tossed.
We cast off, now forever afloat.

Dennis Daly

## ROSARY

Mother, high priestess of beads
Piloting her pajama clad children
Praying for, intoning, heaving
Toward heaven: a consubstantial cure.
Contented, a cumulus carpet of how many?
Ten—finally. One winged away: an emissary.
The glorious mysteries meted
Out in gales of rabbit punches
Around the couch, across side chairs
Each with tabernacle taut
With lessons of locution and fists
That air jab. Counterpoint of voices now rising,
Now falling. A luxury of collected patterns,
A sensor surrounding all called family
Or tribe or blood-bond billeted here.

Loaves of bread, real butter
And milk dust. Frank as food filler
On day's table. All dependent
On these her canny words come
To life, her dimension conquering
Memory sweets and saints. Our father's
Political wins and losses saved us
She said from conflagration
At the Coconut Grove. They were
Meant to be. Her breath becoming
Ours by repetition. A poetic meter
Like fervent Hail Marys, pray
For us—sinners each week, a signal
Of election, a generation,
A heated gush of holy presence.

## CONCUSSION IN WINTER

Deeper into the winter drifts,
The whip and swirl of northeaster
Dropping the branches dead with rot
Onto planes of white pebble-like wash.

Runic messages constructed,
Raised, returned to the alphabetic
Code of self-questioning. We build
A fire on Eagles Hill to feast

In the storm's bright frantic funnel
A burnt sacrifice to winter's
Power, sizzling in tin foil.
Just two of us into the wild,

A boy's adventure, a frozen
Trek away from the pull of parents.
I search for firewood, slip back,
Crack my head, hard ice-flash, shook skull.

I remember the wood, but not
My damn name I joke. Answers do
Not come readily. I leak self,
Walk, listen for my other voice.

## Beth

Tear-torn, keening tower cry
Of mother's loss, the torment
Life-lathering, crib sigh on sigh
Building upward bridge sent, bent

To take her, sister-seraphim
With lip droop, feather shake
Startle of wings in the gray dim
Of antique dawn; she would not wake

Nor eye-roll again. Her pink soft
Spot careful cradled in my arm—
Proud oldest son. Her soul now aloft,
A blink in space, a starry psalm.

## A Bucket of Flounder

Drop lines set a few inches
Off the bottom. My father
And I pulled them up at will,
Thirty or forty flounder

In a day, a few pollock
For chowder. My father cleaned
The fish and I watch, entranced
At the slanted cut across

The fish, the head sliced clean off.
My hands blistering up then
From the worn and splintered
Wooden oars of the rented

Rowboat. My mother would dip
Our fish fillets into corn
Meal and egg. Our grandparents
Would get their share. The neighbors

Next, all wrapped in newspaper.
The sharing of caught-food, no less
A sacrament than priestly
Fare, pulled people together

Beyond need or tribal law,
Matched them in endeavor's yoke
A species rising, not done,
A fishermen's brotherhood.

## Scarlet Fever

My lifelong need for deserts
Began here. I'm eight or so.
Doctor Flynn just arrived. House
Calls by tribal medicine
Men still expected with due
Awe. The Afrika Korps closes
The circle, springs war, traps
Our tank tight to a curled dune.
The sun movie-merciless
On our vehicle's metal.
Temperature rising up,
Lips flaking: one hundred six.
Somewhere an oasis haze
Of ice chips and ginger ale.
Across the sear of blank sand
The tank clanks alive, tracks
Forward under a sun's cruel
Grin. End game shaping, shifting
Anew the final struggle.
Adobe walls do not stop
Santa Ana's men. They meet
Us in the courtyard. I'm with
Crockett, our comrades falling
To insistent bayonets
In this other universe
Of battle heat and bullet
Harm. Bowie's got his guns out
Blasting away already.
I see my dream-fate. I see
It clearly, and then I fade
Into mother's rasp, voice
Of relief: the fever's broke.

## IN THE LIGHT BULB GRAVEYARD

On sunny days the light
Would leap in pink and blue
And blindness, yet still
He climbed and descended
Again, rooting out the shells
Of defective bulbs: brass.

Slung over his left shoulder
He carried a pair of pants,
Chinos tied off at the legs,
Bulging with his flattened
Bounty, carefully culled,
Prospected at the expense

Of an appellative world.
Here at once the dazzle
Of formlessness, where one
Might passively sink,
Fathom after foolish
Fathom, and a desert

Solidified at each moment
By the geometry of
Shifting dunes. Amid
This festival of broken
Glass he made his fortune.

## Dublin Wedding

Mary, the rectory's maid
Ransacked her chest of dresses;
Her work clothes she'll strew in trade.
Hugh, my best man, confesses

His surprise at this honor.
I had just met him. He looked
Like a best man. A butler
By trade. Distinguished. He talked

Sparingly. In the airport
I ducked into a flower
Shop. A bouquet of a sort
That pleases, please. A shower

Of gifts at her feet I'll lay.
No, I told the priest I could
Not afford a wedding day
Ring. Exchanging silver—a good

Alternative, an Irish thing
He said. Your girl's a beauty.
I know I said; on a wing,
A fervent prayer I and she

Promised paltriness of years
Passion's hurt and children's eyes.
Leaving church I paid our fares
On the local bus—no lies

# The Custom House

To our fellow passengers.
She beaming her gown's aura.
I, one of the messengers,
One of the simple fauna,

Took her to a pub; she dined
On hard bread and farmer's cheese.
The center of a refined
World cleaved to her; devotees

Struck, stared at her loveliness.
Past my pint and ham sandwich,
I could see it, did not miss
Her blush—my love, my life's niche.

Dennis Daly

## Leaving Paris

Time taut with over-
Filled knapsacks. That
Split second my hand
Outreached to yours.

Your eyes, the moving
Train, the dash down
The platform, before
We stepped aboard.

There. Never again
Captured that way:
Your silken brown hair,
Innocent veil

Of flawless mystery.
Never again
Exactly that way,
The screech of wheels

On rail in my ears.
The tower gone,
Already the arch missing;
The river Seine,

Flowing on and on,
Becomes your song,
Your love's nascent self,
My heart's nerve line.

The Custom House

## Your Study
*For Colleen*

Your study of what others
Had blueprinted, engineered to alter
The pain of life fading
Much too early, has ended. Plaitlet
Count improvement was the tipoff.
Those blossoming lives
Stolen: one by
One until now until
This time, this silver bullet
Shattered the translucent glass
Barriers of years, broke
The pattern. God's nod,
His not quite smile
Infusing the dying with living fire.
That rarely happens—but it did
On your watch. "Hi Dad,"
You wrote, "it's my study."
And it is yours, and all
Of us, who know you, know it.
A cure's been birthed, eased
From stone into our prism
Of day. It is your study.
And those children of men, who will
Survive are your children,
Are humanity's parents.
In their time they will
Chisel our species anew. It is
Your medical study, overseen
By you. Like a one act
Performance, the lines read

Dennis Daly

Deftly, the personified genetic
Killer falls stricken. Named atypical
Hemolytic uremic syndrome,
He was deadly; he was.
The chorus interrupts
The traffic of the scene, says
In aside to you in the audience
Of science:
This was your study.

## The Violinist
*For Karen*

To be poised by your art
Atop life's intense stage;
The mathematics dart,
Each wave a new message

Of joy, a triumphant
Take of errorless notes
Rising to heaven's bent.
Lover aches, mother dotes:

The action of our hearts
In your instrument's fire,
Sounding in soulful parts
Celestial: a string choir.

Catching light, a dream-
Night of rare reverie,
A creator supreme;
You bow our chords keenly.

## Playing Chess with Jim

Hands handy, you had them then,
Your mathematical head still high,
Muscled; I set up the chessboard,
The beep of the ventilator breathing
Your breaths, stealing your facility
For life-support. You, the good brother,
One of our sisters called you, engage
Me in some special convalescent
Arena, a green jousting field,
A hospital of tactical, twisting
Moves. Pawns ever advancing.
Your face, flickering with mortality,
Blinks: you've lost a step. My knight
Moves in. Life's outlook going grim,
Changed forever as you retreat
Into yourself, recalculate.
A card counter, banned from Vegas,
You banked a family, watched them grow,
Blinked, eye-scanning your work.
Still in the future, your prize
Piece of software there waiting, punched
In by your irises, ALS
be damned. Checked, and checked again.
You seem distracted. I press, read
Your hooded strategy, now gain
The advantage that you've given me,
That you've plotted in each move,
In all the detail of your life's game.

The Custom House

## EPITHALAMIUM
*For Jennifer*

Wedding poems may recall, ritual cornets
On remembered pages, half spun
Gravel passages through dragon thickets--
English garden formal. But the keel-hauled sun,

Breathless above us in the Aral Sea,
Urges another meter: you tour the ship
On the basin floor with no timidity,
Tug at your camera, shoot a frame, sip

Bottled water from where? Life's like that.
You take your chances, but act you must
With what's available. You had it down pat
When I peeked in and heard your gust

Of poetry whistling from the lectern
At Saint A's, brusquely read, pouring through the crowd
Of admirers. Or ambushed in dream-like turn
By teen soldiers in the Chatkal Mountains. I vowed

Never again to put you in jeopardy
Until carjacked by militia fishermen,
North of Nukus. Then a lamp-bound genie
Touched us all with fugue-like years. You and Ben

Now queue up for fate and family and fortune
I'm to give you away? Not likely, my wealth,
My oldest daughter, my satellite moon.
To you and your Ben, deep love and denim health.

Dennis Daly

## Philoctetes' Foot

For years now I've watched the symphony
Of weather soar and drop and whistle.
I've composed in my head a man free
To pray in wind and rain, a missal

Filled with etched and numinous totems
Of time's tears and lost initiatives
Meditated on, a set of problems
Overlaid. What takes? What gives?

My foot oozes the reason I'm here,
Exiled, marooned, living by arrow
And bow. A multiple of birds fear,
For I never miss, suck the marrow

Each morning on my bed of soft leaves.
Soon I'll leave, meet their boats at anchor,
Face the cure, a comfort that believes
In words, the miracle of wonder.

## THE CATCH
*For Patrick*

The bat's crack
Told all. I sat
In a soundless
Car, felt the hover
Over left center
Field, tensed
As Pat— his first
Play as a little
Leaguer—backed
Up, near, very
Near the fence,
Watched the descent,
The dive of ball
To earth, like
The fate of all
Of us, his glove
Now poised, a moment
Of absolute pretense,
The arc extending
To the lip of the fence,
Falling like a photon,
Piercing space, stopped
The ins and outs of breaths,
My lungs curling, aping
His glove. The soft
Oil-worked leather
Comforts a smack,
A blind catch,
A game always won
In the evergreen
Of a boy's summer
On life's endless
Baseball field.

# PEACE

There is in solitude a gnawing peace
Not found in the eye-center of mob crush.
There is an ease of mood in tumult of pain,
A fading into sleep as whole and complete
As the bud and flower of universe:
The begetting of our heaven and our hell.

Even as our elaboration of hell
Respires from a self-absorbing peace
To curtain with horror our universe,
The sun returns like God's face to crush
The intrusions of shadow, make complete
Light's canticles despite obtruding pain.

In our intimate lives of strophic pain
We create our demons, summon them from hell,
Set the narrative, so total, so complete
That it shudders our corporal self, our peace-
Of-mind. We retreat from detrusion and crush
To safer ground, to a public universe.

Here among the bricks and stones of universe
We face the outwardness, the armies of pain
Not obscured within the enormous crush
Of humanity. These forces from hell
Are faced; and the totemic word of peace
Intoned, but unmeasured, not near complete.

Man's pride like Babel, unrestrained and un-complete.
Harmony disturbed in this universe:
Clashing of hosts, damning of what was peace.
Paralyzed sensations, a shock without pain
Allows the artist freedom in hell
To create his object, to sunder, to crush.

The Custom House

It satisfies the ancient need to crush.
The failure of rebellion must be complete
As if we abolished the precepts of hell
From this newer, renovated universe,
A haven from pleasure and likely pain.
But is this victory a conquest for peace?

In the very core of this universe
Beyond the known attributes that define pain,
Here in our heart's turmoil, finally— unloosed peace.

Dennis Daly

## FRANCIS

The quiet accumulation of comfort,
Somehow you evaded its ownership
When, on the curve and dip

Of a bird's wing, you crossed the dreadful
Wall to what you were; and there, among
The green swords, you let a young

Life, as hot as an autumn sap, flow
Inward, underneath your iron skin,
Around your gentle heart; the din

Was terrifying. In the midst of this
You sang of a bleeding creation
Where words, like leaves, tumble in the sun.

The Custom House

# CHASING THE MOON

Swept along the backstreets of space, we stalk the moon,
The mewling magician of light, the jostler of moods.
Your arms thrown about my neck, anchoring me
To your heart-seed of awe: the gravity and thrill,
The danger of this game life; we take the corner
Much too fast at thirty. I brake, knowing better.
You glimpse it again at the next three-deckered turn:
A momentary hover, a whirling blizzard
Topping a telephone pole, like a pinwheel.
Then, indrawn into the symmetry of an oak's grief,
It floats out, eyes red, limning another gable.
Both of us, brimmed with laughter, blow a kiss,
Conspire a simple rhythm, a child's playful concoction
To this strangely singular, compelling vision,
This messenger from the near past, who sprints above us now
Busting open a fragile cloud like a lion
Through a paper hoop. I veer to the right, accelerate
Up a hill. "There it is!" we both shout out loud,
Lounging for a second, softening the black seascape
With a dappled highway of gold fleck—then on and on
It scribs over the ceaseless waves churning in
From that vanishing point of all hope and becoming.

## CAESARIAN BIRTH

Events vacillate in the blackness
Of this pre-world, a narrative
Illuminated by silver waves,
Shooting-stars, and lightning's turbulence.

Gazing on these portents in wonder,
The tug lessens, the urgency fades
As a thought swims toward the soul's center,
The heart-press, the nurturer of all.

The intrusion, like a shock of ice,
A freezing of the polar seas;
And the blistering from this knowledge
Destroying sure harmony, haven.

Hiding under a vital tuck,
She curls away from the life-giver,
The alien hand that draws, delivers
Through time's widening tear her song of self.

The Custom House
## FALLSTAFF REMINISCES

My life in exile coming to a close;
Only the grave waits—the glutton of eyes.
Henry, my Henry, awakened from a dream
Of surfeit, his nature he falsifies.

Or if not: what once was, now has vanished;
The prankster metamorphisized, twisted
Into a king, his friends dismissed from service,
Even his mentor—myself—blacklisted.

There's your justice! While he needed us
To show him the comedy of vice,
He wore his mask well: a drunkard of promise,
A bawd, a thief in paradise.

But now, in spite of that, he climbs to heights
Of fantasy: the brave knight, who conquers Gaul;
His friends—too fat, too old, too weak
To change. Nor would they—all in all.

Dennis Daly

## Mermaid's Purse

Packet of skate floundering
On the foaming margin between sea
And land, or stiff rubbish left

By the ambivalent tide;
I touch you like the pages
Of an ancient book, respecting

The guise of your fragility.
You seem not quite a nest, untied
And left to drift, nor a womb

Discarded after usefulness
Abruptly ceased, but a husk
Of some minor sea-god

Isolated, idealized,
With no creations left.

The Custom House

## "I Thought All for the Best"

Just a perspective: a wry turn
Of blue on a beach sky, remnants
Of the razor clam bleached by
An hysterical sun, east the gull
Flies, thick gruel still dripping from
Its satisfied bill.

Or a performance: the hermit
Crab, that sly impersonator
Hidden away in a moon shell
Greets me with one claw. Faker!
My feet wince, pierced by dune wheat
Sprouting pale. This is no place for love.
No, not even contour fences
To contain the cynical sand, preserve
The dunes. Leave them to their own
Enemies: wind and sea.

The intervening hand, the naïve
Embrace, the bluest I've ever
Seen the sky. I want to tell you.
O Mercutio, Mercutio.

Dennis Daly

## Vertigo

Everywhere the dust of a solid existence
Bellowing up at you. Beings smashed apart
Like powdered rock: faces of atoms, of chance
Arrangements, of unfinished men, who come and depart
Offering every choice. Commit yourself! Commit!
A voice around you curls, cozens from your shadow
World: anything you want, pleasures to fit.
You hesitate. Stop.
                    Standing before the window,
Your face disintegrates. The street, bulging
With refugees, whispers its temptation. A fuse
Burns faster. Which of a thousand different ways,
You ask. And already they're past. The clues
That you followed have disappeared. But the maze
Still remains: there is no choice worth choosing.

The Custom House

## NIGHT CAFÉ
*After Van Gogh*

Rolling back the stone,
Sucked in sitting
At the nearest table—
Thinking it your first

Ambulance ride. Drugged
In absinthes, left
In abeyance—tick tock
He'll be alright.

Watch the clock—
Reds oozing, greens
Pumping down on you,
Yellows enough to

Sicken. The smell of
An obese rat
Dead of his very
Obesity—

His testicles
Crushed. Christ just
Finished a game of
Billiards listens

To scuffling beyond
The rock, which back
In place is only that:
Back in place.

## Moon Path

The draw, the draw is everything.
Sooner or later the cold clear
Moon offers a way, a springboard
For those of us who, stranded
After a hard day of talk and smile—
The usual dreariness, want out.

From the seawall you can see them
Already, tip-toeing above
The surf, following the flicker
Of constant path; the wet sea-doors
Below them magically shut
As tight as a frozen ice-field.

"There's mine! There's mine!" Someone shouts.
But they pay no heed, shimmering,
Blending into their element.
As they become more tangible,
We fade, our colors flowing over
Concrete wall, mixing with the tide.

After our lives end, and the earth
Brakes to a crash, there they are:
Naked, reveling in the blackness
Of their other world—specters
Hurling down a highway of light,
Just as we left them.

The Custom House

## Night Crawlers

After the rain of evening ends its darkest rage
And weather twins, their task completed, leave the stage,
Primeval crawlers out from hidden dens arrayed
On hopeless islets, cumbered flesh that waits abeyed
For fishermen with cans, which for this night were found
To scoop up from the slime (that is, unless they've drowned)
This ancient kind; and those, who in the morn are left
To find another shelter, will forget the theft.

## New World

I woke this morning, all had changed.
My kin folk gone; my children aged.
And all the world seemed so estranged.

The trees, my friends, went off deranged.
Wild things broke loose, un-zooed, not caged.
I woke this morning, all had changed.

The sheep, the yaks, the beasts that ranged
On field, on hill, knelt down, outraged.
And all the world seemed so estranged.

Flying fish and seabirds then arranged
To meet mid-flight—not ever staged!
I woke this morning, all had changed.

I breathed in still, my lungs exchanged
Un-equilibrium I gauged.
And all the world seemed so estranged.

The moon ignored, the sun shortchanged.
Our gods are otherwise engaged.
I woke this morning, all had changed.
And all the world seemed so estranged.

## III. INDUSTRIAL SONNETS

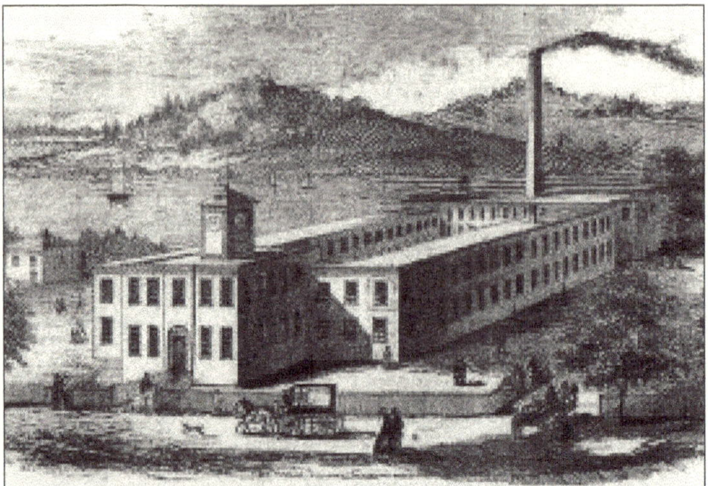

The Custom House

## In Building 30

In building 30 they bear no details
Admit no fragile hand, no subtle stroke;
Here the long screech and clatter of metal
Encompass with context, sometimes shatter.

Nearsighted in the inner workings,
The outer rim illusive, men move
Among the many planes without comfort
Of recognizable shape.

Parallel to the concrete floor, a plate
Of iron barges through the vault, chained
To a girder. Below, a huddle

Of workers — next shift, they finish their coffee,
Ignore the crane's siren with scornful looks,
Spit out the grit of conversation.

Dennis Daly

## Retirement

One day before his retirement,
Crouched over, pacified by the years,
He cannot believe what has ended,
Nor remember another past.

Most of his friends dead or gone elsewhere,
He shakes my hand; I hadn't known him,
Always pitied that frail man
With gray blotchy skin, a cloth skullcap

And expressionless face fixed under it,
Not quite comic. He spray-painted
Pipes and parts of curious machinery

In his three-walled room at the track's end.
Tomorrow he'll surprise: washed and well-dressed,
Solitary, he'll mimic almost pure form.

The Custom House

## THE BENCH HAND

Tapping through into the atmosphere
Of clatter and high pitch, of emery rolls
And shooting sparks, the bench hand hammers
A well-clamped curved rib into place.

The piece, contracted by liquid oxygen,
Fits easily, expands as it warms.
He glances at his blueprints, reaches
For another tool as he does each day

Puzzling together the contraptions
Of human kind. His thoughts, set within their system,
Flush against the usual constraints,

Collapse into themselves, become the object,
The metallic piece. He seeks out the burrs,
The imperfections. Expunges them.

Dennis Daly

## The Foreman

The foreman peers into the predicament
Of skin and blood, seeks the bits of rebellion
Once adjunctive to himself. He assigns
Work, causes in his way ad hoc cohesion.

Climbing up on a mill, caustic, careful
To a point, he directs another's hand.
They hate him for this: the sureness of his voice,
The authority, the power to cut loose.

He steals their leisure, invokes furious rules
Of industry, sneers at their little escapes,
Their ridiculous dreams of revenge.

Both feeding from them and repelled by them,
He fends them off like distant relatives,
Embarrassments he had hoped to outgrow.

The Custom House
## SECURITY GUARDS

They watch us closely, suspect the truth
In our easy swagger. We are the thieves
Who conspire to steal from under them
The solidity of their futures.

Our cars are combed, company phones bugged.
Even our lunch pails eyed as carriers
Of possible contraband. We are searched
At random for chisels or screwdrivers

Or other more exotic tools. Cameras
Of the most modern type record every move,
Isolate in a moment the ringleaders

Of our cause. Yet they cannot stop us.
Piece by piece we'll pocket our workplace.
Secure it. Then commission the guards.

Dennis Daly

## THE OIL FARM

A thick lifeless gruel curdles in these drums,
A poison of unnatural substance
Needed to salve the meta-machinery,
Which built of rigid parts, alters others.

Without it to lubricate or cleanse
Paralysis appears like a genie,
A malevolent wizard who freezes
At wand's touch our stations of power.

Multicolored they settle on three tiers of racks,
Hundreds of them—rusted and dented,
Leaking in the gaudiness of sunlight.

Their fumes of intoxication murmer
Into our mild breaths a heaviness
As insoluble as halted tears.

The Custom House

## THE FORK LIFT

It lurches forward from the Mesozoic
Of V-bay bellowing black exhaust,
A grimy prehistoric beast, an engine
Laboring in the mists of a turbine's birth.

Now lowers its elevated burden
Before the throng of assembled chippers,
Who peer with inquisitive insect-eyes
Into an already benched silver trunnion.

Withdrawing its tusks from the pallet,
Wood splintering, the fork lift retreats,
Driven down the dimly lit oil-caked aisles

Through the knots and numberless barriers
Of this transitional network; its task
To piece together, to pull into being.

Dennis Daly

## THE STEWARD

They can't pin him down, suspend, or dismiss him
Without trouble; a political fury,
A resentment almost feudal would pulse
Through these workers, the power- famished ones.

He's ruined pieces—too many of them!
Pulled himself out, hurting with back problems,
The recurrent industrial accident,
To visit Cuba, Iran, China.

Not content with the usual grievance:
Poor performance warning, short-changed pay check,
He'd set up a foreman, humiliate him

In front of his peers. There are rumors:
Party member or company plant?
His own partisans have hedged their bets.

The Custom House

## ELECTION NIGHT AT UNION HALL

Rumors like thick dangerous vapors
Burst to fire, explode from their reasoned forms.
Enormous men with bloated fingers
Wield their knives, scrape the backs of ballots.

In quantum motions a computer
Pours out little sums of retribution
Or cheap listless "thanks"; that reward
Yanked from the indifferent favor-gobblers.

We mill about, exchange a nervous glance,
Demagogues all—brave opportunists
Manipulated by others; we return

The favor, taste a tyrant's power, pull
Those grubby heart strings, then deliver, withhold.
Now, loosed from a bullhorn, drone the numbers.

Dennis Daly

## The Welder

Numinous as fire from the burning bush
Below Horeb, the blue light tremors
Above the welder like a nimbus
Electric with substance, chafing to be.

We watch this melting of boundary,
This craft of connection with averted eyes
That cannot see beyond our own soft lights
Harsher mornings, hothouses of almost.

Behind his dark- glassed helmet he delves
Into the varied trons of metal,
Unburdened by his torch's discharge.

In this realm of repair and renew
A man can glimpse the depths of his future
And the rises, the virtual life beyond.

The Custom House
## TOOL KEEPERS

Some would have you believe in an essence
Beyond words, existing as the heart
Of a thing. Our tool keepers tell us,
In their tempered way, a different story.

They dole out the utensils, what workers use
To chip away, mold, or combine matter.
And what they cannot alter, they measure
To a new definition, a new meaning.

It's these creations, refined again and again
Into chiseled hierarchies, that obscure
By levels, leading the way, civilizing.

The originals, if there were any,
Disappear finally, machine-shredded,
Generated into redundancy.

Dennis Daly

## The Auditors

The system calculates itself, crawls
With office people, clipboard carriers
Reeking of musk. They peer into tubs
Of brightly colored dye, climb racks four tiers high

Sniffing out reels of synthetic tape;
Then move on, leave behind a trail
Dotted with discarded carbon sheets,
Barrels of resin still to be weighed.

Despite doubts: a sugaring of cartons
Half-filled or empty, an obsolete shape
Extruded and packed under pretense,

Their subtotals, cantankerous at first,
Flourish, demand a justification
Never quite found in two dimensions.

The Custom House

## TIME CLOCK

Always we line up early: ten minutes
To go—a guarantee in the matter
Of some small choice. We grimace gossip,
Curses, quips. Exchange lies about home.

Each fingers his card (some mangle it),
Examines the name as if for the first time,
And its corresponding number. The clock
Clicks again, a new digit appears.

Waiting, propped against a dreary wall,
We stand in a twilight between our dreams
And what we most assuredly are.

Eyes meet, dissolve into this rhythm:
A tightening of the discontinuous.
The buzzer sounds. One by one we punch out.

## Piece Work

There's money in it if you're willing to work,
To become something other than what you are:
Whether wrapping copper rods with tape,
Trimming hides, or boring a valve cover.

No longer an entity, but an act,
An energy, which cancels the clock's
Distressing measure and leaps hell-bent
Past hesitation, beyond every comma.

You side with those, who bank on accomplishment,
The quantity altered, the sweetness
Of result, like a piece of furniture

Just finished, lacquered, almost universal
In its solidity. Here the artisan,
Pulsing into his object, begins to fade.

The Custom House

## IN THE SCRAP YARD

Between barrels of metal cutouts
And broken office cabinets, he sets
The pallet of bronze gears, their glisten
Dulled by storage, caked with oil and soot.

To move a turbine, their pre-empted function
Lost to industry, lost like a verse,
An ancient's words used to stuff
A bestial shape, the counterfeit crocodile.

The well-made fragments, unused or unseen,
Reinterpret their out-of-synch meanings,
Center themselves, gather in their background.

These parts give birth, beget a measured whole,
A precision cut in our mortal craft.
He abandons them to this chaos.

Dennis Daly

## Unemployment Line

Idle hands, excused by the powers
Of organization, without that pattern
That focuses on or integrates one to
His object, are the devil's workshop.

They wait, shuffle, look for a familiar grin.
Some, the embarrassed, glance downward, peer
Into the mysteries of waxed, scuffled tile.
Each sees his check, cashed and already spent.

After answering the expected questions
With engaging but concocted stories
Of applications, they pick up and leave

Past the gray and pudgy office faces,
Paroled into the cool bliss of sunshine
With energy too diffuse for profit.

## LOVERS ABOVE THE RESIN SILOS

Climbing upward through a child's bewilderment:
His fear of altitude, or being let loose
To fall forever; he leaps up the ladder
To where she laughs on the sun-strafed platform.

They let down the weighted measuring line,
Delving into the unastonished absence
Until it finds a floor, a solid plane
Of resin pellets, dispelling all doubts.

Their clothes tossed aside before the weather twin
Plays his mischievous surprise, soaks them
With a shock of soft enveloping rain.

Here he sees her—Beauty—as only he could,
A fragileness between the necessities
Of two always encroaching strata.

## WILDCAT STRIKE

Momentum binds with angry shudders
And righteous nods that awaken within each
Of them the fractious, the fraise-encircled
Stronghold of center, of noble self.

They peel away from their grounded machines,
Revved up by rebel stewards. The break
Carries them, complects their grievances
Into an exhilaration of whole cloth.

Apostate-defiant, with every step
They march doggedly into the lighter sphere
Of sudden glee and red gonfalon,

Compelling authority to a certain pretense,
An answer of identifiable scrawl
As personal as a signature.

The Custom House

## OVERTIME

Within us the hidden destructive note
Lies quietly, flexing its potential.
We gamble with our allotted moments:
The necessities of the corporal,

The banalities of territory
Perplexing us—we all have a price,
A premium to use or disuse
For bread, beer, and other more eccentric bets.

Some just bank it, a resolute prayer
Of speculation, an agreement
That what works, will continue to the point

Of payoff, an annual interest
Compounded and compounded again
As our surrender is to the corporate will.

## Maintenance

Surgeons they enter the aging skin, the bone,
The sinew with a faith, a self-reliant knowledge
Of irrefutable power. What exists
Fails, finds rebirth in their determined hands.

As they finger through buildings and machines,
Isolate the severed bolt, the frayed wire,
We watch them, amazed at their selfless touch,
Their intimacy with an alien essence.

A few will disappear, identified
Into their objects; their offspring, grease-tufted
Factory-bred cats, claw, cut past us

Towards creation's rational fringe. We see
Them through the widening tears of this fabric,
Through the gaps that we pretend make sense.

The Custom House

## ASBESTOS

None of us wear masks or are told why
We shovel and sweep this gray material
Into neat piles, then seal it in plastic.
But of course we know by its texture

What it is and pin the right name on it.
Manic, we joke about our final moments:
Sniff, collapse, stiffen—our fantasies
Of death, always curious, play themselves out.

Like children we urge each other on
To disaster: the acceptance of the dare
More exhilarating when our end

(though at this moment remote) becomes
A common plight. Prompted by un-casual friends
We'll pale about this in years to come.

Dennis Daly

## Benefits

Such favors give a certain magnitude:
So much per pound, a price tag
Slung about our big toe. We are secure,
Our limbs are safe, each misfortune assures us.

The hospital, like a multi-tiered repair shop,
Stands ready—they know we're backed by cash.
Even in our death-dream, the desk-girl
Smiles, nods us in with no undue problem.

When the toluene-covered worker
Burnt up at the touch of a single spark
From her too-electric underclothes,

She must have thought with some satisfaction
And a not unwarranted smugness
On her choice of plans, "Thank God I'm covered."

The Custom House

## Drill Smoke

A decent sort, pleasant, incompetent,
He accepted an "inability"
Six months later, which demoted him.
We talked all that night in his alcove.

Kicking aside the rigid curls, the scraps
Of his trade, I climbed on his pocked bench,
Leaned against his tool crate and watched
As his drill pierced through a relenting metal

Sending wisps of smoke past the long snout
Of his oil can. Self-taught, he flunked a language course
At some sleazy night school, which hurt him

Beyond consolation. Even then he spouted
Dark slogans of nothing-to-lose; now he waits,
Like other hurt creatures, for his chance.

## Gear Plant Gate

These transitory shapes pour from the deepest,
The most profound shadows of our workplace.
They pass over the continuance
Of railway tracks, leaving a silent wake:

Dimmed buildings, rising steam, the frigid moon.
Scuffing along toward their exit vehicles,
They bristle with new life, anticipate
A distant necessity, an endless need

Both competitive and desperate.
One boasts the sweetness of an agile bedmate,
Another belts down a swig of whiskey,

The primer, the first of a night-long drunk.
There's a dampness just up from the river;
It slivers in, portends a fitful sleep.

The Custom House

## THE CARBOLOY INSERT

In my dark alcove I carve enormous valves
The shrieks are not mine, nor the pain. I wear
Slowly: harder than other metals.
And as for precision—near perfect. They pressed

Me into being from carbon and soft steel:
Minute particles adhering without bond
To an idea. A seeking of form
And finding it. O brittleness! Bathed in coolant,

Set for the correct depth, my cut neither strays
Nor falters. At contact chips are shot like darts
Or piercing verbs. Clamped, I speak a physics

To the world without. My composition
Includes machinist. He watches, listens,
Creates—all according to my nature.

Dennis Daly

## Layoff

Hit, sculptured livelihoods gone,
Their union's bunker-line impotent,
Beyond useless. "What do we pay
You for—if not times like these?"

Their questions unanswerable.
The manager sips his whiskey comfort,
A worker takes the stool next to him,
Snarls in hatred, pulls a gun.

"You've wrecked my life." "No I tried
To keep you, you're one of the good ones,"
He answered, it's the union guy

That's in control." He pocketed the gun,
Left. The bartender called me in time;
I fled my office down the side stairs.

The Custom House

## Rat-Friend

Doubled your money, didn't you?
Yes, you admitted it to me. "I'm
A whore," you said. That doesn't
Excuse what you did, your betrayals.

You were clever, plotted with us,
A tempered representative
Of your fellow workers. A piece-
Worker on paper, reporting

Every decision of ours to your handlers.
My home under surveillance for six
Months and you, my good friend, my erstwhile

Ally. I stood on pallets next
To you campaigning, laughed at your wit,
At your wry disturbing ironies.

## The Electrician

He knew things, listened to wires
Buzz above us, renewed connections
Or broke them off. Every liquid lunch
He fueled up and flamed with fervor.

Funneling information to me—
My trusted friend—his soul sparked
At screwdriver contact, creating
A myth costumed in pads, helmeted

In hard plastic to face down enmity
Of undetonated bile set to go off
On the weight of my step. He believed

In wonder, showed me the bugged phones
And gadget traps, his fear-cord still frayed.
He generated whatever I became.

The Custom House

**DENNIS DALY** was born in Salem Massachusetts. He graduated from Boston College with a B.S. degree and earned a Master of Arts degree at Northeastern University. At Northeastern he studied poetry under Samuel French Morse.

For ten years Dennis worked for the General Electric Company. He became a union activist and was elected into the leadership of the 9000 member Local 201 of the International Union of Electrical Workers. During this period he published and edited The Union Activist and the North Shore Union Leader. He also was the managing editor of the Electrical Union News.

Dennis has been published in numerous magazines and small poetry journals such as Dark Horse, The Sou'wester, Lyric, Boston Today Magazine, Soundings East, Tendril, Poetry &, Green House, Lyrical Somerville, Wilderness House Literary Review, The Istanbul Literary Review, and The Muddy River Poetry Review and is included with two other poets in a chapbook entitled 10 X 3, published by Northeastern University Press. He reads his poems regularly at Stone Soup Poetry and the Walnut Street Coffee Cafe in Lynn and is a member of the Bagel Bards, a group of poets, who meet weekly in Somerville.

In addition Dennis has published travel articles and many op-ed pieces in the Salem Evening News. He is currently working on another book of poetry.

Dennis lives in Salem Massachusetts with his wife, Joanne. They have four adult children.